The storm shall not wake thee, nor shark overtake thee,
Asleep in the arms of the slow-swinging seas.

—Rudyard Kipling

PHOTO CREDITS:

pp. 4–5, 21: © Mark Conlin; p. 6: © 1988 Doug Perrine; pp. 9, 10, 25: © Norbert Wu; p. 13: © Ron and Valerie Taylor; p. 14: © Mike Nolan; pp. 17, 22: © Doug Perrine; p. 18: © 1979 Tom McHugh, the National Audubon Society Collection; p. 26: © Doc White/Images Unlimited, Inc.; p. 29: © James D. Watt/Innerspace Visions; p. 30: Rosemary Chastney/Ocean Images, Inc.

The name of the Smithsonian, Smithsonian Institution and the sunburst logo are registered trademarks of the Smithsonian Institution.

Collins is an imprint of HarperCollins Publishers.

Library of Congress Cataloging-in-Publication Data
Simon, Seymour.
Sharks / Seymour Simon.
p. cm.
ISBN-10: 0-06-087712-X (trade bdg.) — ISBN-13: 978-0-06-087712-5 (trade bdg.)
ISBN-10: 0-06-087713-8 (pbk.) — ISBN-13: 978-0-06-087713-2 (pbk.)
1. Sharks—Juvenile literature. [1. Sharks.] I. Title.
QL638.9.S56 1995   95-1593
597'.31—dc20   CIP
                                                      AC

4 5 6 7 8 9 10
❖
Revised Edition

Smithsonian Mission Statement

For more than 160 years, the Smithsonian has remained true to its mission, "the increase and diffusion of knowledge." Today the Smithsonian is not only the world's largest provider of museum experiences supported by authoritative scholarship in science, history, and the arts but also an international leader in scientific research and exploration. The Smithsonian offers the world a picture of America, and America a picture of the world.

Natural History Mission Statement

We inspire curiosity, discovery, and learning about nature and culture through outstanding research, collections, exhibitions, and education.

It never fails. You're at the ocean, swimming in the surf, and someone pretends to be a shark. They sing ominous music and then lunge at you.

People have always made up myths and legends about creatures they find mysterious and terrifying. Sensationalized books, television shows, and movies strengthen the myth that sharks are always on the lookout to attack people. The truth is that there are fewer than 100 shark attacks worldwide each year, and most victims live to tell their stories. In fact, you have a better chance of being hit by lightning than of being attacked by a shark. Sharks have killed fewer people in the United States in the past one hundred years than are killed in automobile accidents over a single holiday weekend. And no shark in the world counts people as part of its regular dinner menu.

When you know the truth about sharks, you'll begin to see them as the fascinating creatures they are, instead of the monsters of myth.

Sharks are fish, but they are very different from most fish. They belong to a class of fish known as Chondrichthyes (kon-DRIK-thees). The name comes from the Greek words *chondros*, which means cartilage, and *ichthyus*, which means fish. Like all fish, sharks have backbones and teeth, but unlike other fish, sharks have no other bones. Their skeletons are made of cartilage, a tough, white, flexible material, just like the stuff at the end of your nose and in your ears.

Like most fish, sharks breathe through gills. But while most fish have one pair of gills, sharks have five to seven, as you can see on this Caribbean reef shark. Most fish don't have eyelids, but some kinds of sharks have three of them for each eye. Two are like yours, an upper and lower eyelid. The third eyelid is transparent. It covers the entire eye and protects it.

Sharks also lack the swim bladder that keeps most bony fish afloat. A swim bladder is like a balloon inside a fish's body that keeps it buoyant. Sharks keep from sinking because there is oil in their livers that acts like a float, and also because they keep swimming. If a shark stops swimming, its weight pulls it down to the bottom. Scientists calculate that sharks cruise at about one to three miles per hour. A few kinds can suddenly speed through the water at up to 40 miles per hour.

Most people think of jaws and teeth when they think of sharks, and with good reason. Many sharks do have powerful jaws and rows of sharp teeth. Some sharks can bite nearly 300 times harder than a human, enough to cut through a thick piece of steel. Sharks may lose a tooth when they bite something hard, but they never run out of new teeth. A shark's jaw is lined with as many as twenty rows of teeth, one behind the other. When a shark breaks or loses a tooth, another one moves forward to replace it. Some sharks replace their teeth one by one, while others replace an entire row at the same time. A shark may go through thousands of teeth during its life.

The tiger shark, shown here, is common along the east coast of North America. Nicknamed the garbage-can shark, it will eat anything it can swallow, including bits of food, car license plates, and cans of paint. But with its strong, sharp teeth it will also attack other sharks, sea turtles, rays, seabirds, and even the occasional human being.

No two kinds of sharks have exactly the same kind of teeth. Bottom-dwelling sharks, such as the nurse shark, usually have broad, flat teeth for crushing crabs and other shellfish. Fast-swimming sharks, such as the mako and great white, who hunt in the open sea, have sharp teeth for cutting up other sharks, marine mammals, and big fish. But with all these teeth, sharks don't chew their food. If the prey is small enough, a shark swallows it whole. If the prey is too big, a shark uses its teeth to tear it apart and then swallows the parts.

Three of the largest sharks in the world have the smallest teeth compared to their body size. The whale shark (shown here), basking shark, and megamouth shark are called filter-feeders. They swim near the surface with their mouths open. As the water flows through their gills, they strain out small animals called plankton. These sharks have hundreds of tiny teeth, each smaller than the thickness of a pencil.

Even a shark's skin has teeth! A shark's body is covered with rough skin that feels like sandpaper and with little skin-teeth called denticles (DENT-uh-culs). You can cut yourself by rubbing against a shark's skin.

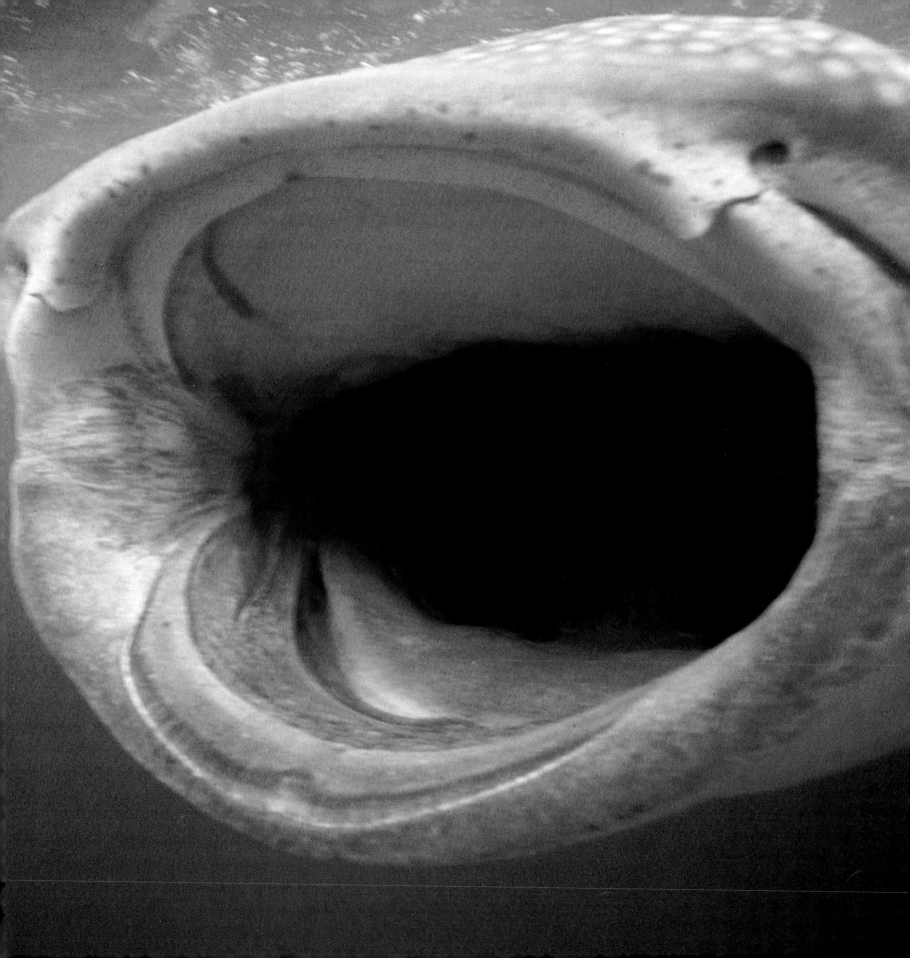

Most sharks are cold-blooded. This means that the temperature of a shark's body depends upon the temperature of the water around it. Most sharks live in temperate or tropical ocean waters, while only some inhabit the colder polar seas. One way scientists categorize sharks is by the temperature of the water in which they live.

Different kinds of sharks are adapted to different temperatures, so as the water temperature changes with the seasons, many sharks migrate. For example, sharks that live in the Northern Hemisphere may travel farther north in the summer to find cooler water and travel south toward warmer water in the winter.

Some sharks travel great distances. One blue shark (like the one shown here) was tagged in the waters off New York City and then found months later off the coast of Brazil, 3,700 miles away.

A shark's six (yes, six!) senses make it one of the best hunters in the world. Because sound travels five times faster and farther in water than on land, hearing is the first sense that alerts a shark to its prey. Sharks' inner ears are sensitive to low-frequency sounds. They can hear a wounded fish thrashing in the water from as much as 3,000 feet away.

As the shark swims toward the sound, it may come across an odor path that flows in a current from the prey. Sharks are like "swimming noses," and can detect even tiny amounts of blood in the water. The shark's ability to smell seems to increase as it gets hungrier. Reef sharks that had been deprived of food in experiments were able to smell as little as one drop of fish blood in a large tankful of water. Given this, it's not so surprising to learn that half of a shark's brain is devoted to its sense of smell.

Beneath the ocean's surface it is not easy to see, since the water is often cloudy and dim. But a shark's eyes are well suited to this underwater world. In the back of a shark's eye is a mirrorlike surface called a tapetum lucidum. The tapetum reflects light back through the eye and helps the shark to see in dim light. Light bouncing off the tapetum makes some sharks' eyes seem to glow in the dark, like cats' eyes, as you can see with this tiger shark.

Sharks have two kinds of touch that aid them in locating prey. One kind is like the sense of touch you have when you feel whether something is hot or cold or rough or smooth. The shark also uses a kind of "distant" touch. This distant touch allows the shark to sense the vibrations of an object long before it comes into contact with it. The blacktip reef shark pictured here could have tracked the mackerel from as much as 600 feet away, by sensing its vibrations.

The shark's ability to do this comes from its lateral lines, rows of small pores that run along the shark's sides, stretching from its head to its tail. When a fish swims nearby, it causes small movements in the water. The shark's lateral lines sense the movement, and the shark can find the fish, even if it cannot see it.

An extra "sixth" sense, called electroreception, helps some sharks to locate prey they cannot find with their other senses. Sharks have hundreds of tiny pores in their heads and lower jaws called the ampullae of Lorenzini. (Lorenzini was the name of the seventeenth-century scientist who first described them.) The shark's ampullae pick up the small electrical signals that all living animals give off. The electrical signals guide the shark to its prey at close range. Sharks have the most sensitive electrical organs of any known animal.

Many bony fish reproduce through external fertilization. The female fish deposits many small eggs in the water, which are then fertilized by the male. Unlike most bony fish, all sharks reproduce through internal fertilization, as mammals and birds and reptiles do. However, once the eggs are fertilized inside the female shark, they develop in several different ways, depending on the species of shark.

Some sharks, such as horn sharks, nurse sharks, and cat sharks, lay their fertilized eggs on the ocean floor. Each egg is enclosed in a case or shell just before it is laid, and the case becomes attached to rocks or seaweed. Horn sharks screw their egg cases into cracks between rocks or sunken pieces of wood. When the eggs are first laid, they are soft and pale. The cases harden in a few hours into tough, leathery shells that protect the developing eggs. The photograph shows a swell shark emerging from its egg case. The six-inch-long baby shark, or pup, took about eight months to hatch. Shark pups hatch in six to fifteen months, depending on the species. Sharks that lay eggs are called oviparous.

Most kinds of sharks keep the developing eggs inside their bodies and then give birth to live young. Each shark lives off a yolk until it is ready to hatch. In one kind of shark the developing young are cannibals, feeding first on yolks, and then on one another. The female sand tiger shark has a double uterus, and, by the time the pups are ready to be born, there will be only two pups left—one in the female's right uterus, the other in the left. Sharks that give birth to live young from eggs that have developed in their bodies, including the tiger, mako, and thresher sharks, are called ovoviviparous.

In a few kinds of sharks, such as the lemon, hammerhead, and blue, each fertilized egg develops separately inside a small egg sac. The pups receive food and oxygen from the mother through an umbilical cord. The young sharks are born live in litters ranging from two to twenty. The photo shows the birth of a lemon shark. The tail of the pup is still wrapped in the egg sac. Sharks that give birth in this fashion are called viviparous.

Newborn pups make easy prey for other sharks, so female sharks go to areas where sharks don't usually live to give birth. The mother might be tempted to eat her own pups, but she is inhibited from eating during the birthing period. This is the extent of the mother's nurturing, though; sharks don't care for their young after birth.

There are about 350 kinds of sharks, which seems like a lot until you learn that there are more than 20,000 kinds of bony fish. Researchers know that there are other kinds of sharks not yet discovered.

Sharks come in many different sizes, shapes, and colors. A full-grown dwarf shark is as small as your mom's hand, and a whale shark is longer than a school bus. Most sharks have slender, torpedo-shaped bodies and long, pointed snouts. But some sharks have short, broad snouts and tails, and others have very flat bodies and fins. There are brown sharks and blue sharks and sharks with polka dots, like this cat shark. Some have strange-looking heads, and others have strange-looking tails.

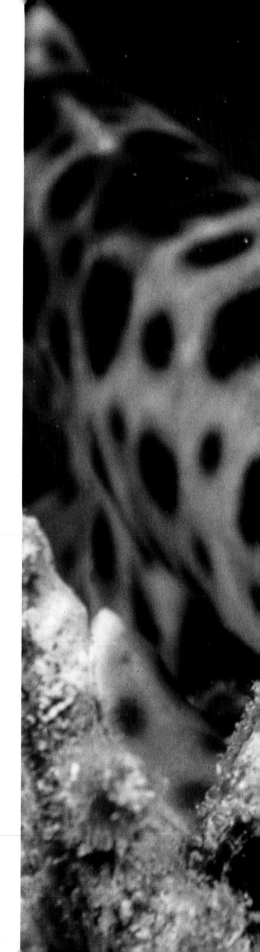

The largest shark, and indeed the largest fish in the world, is the whale shark. It can grow as long as sixty feet and weigh as much as twenty tons—as long and heavy as a huge trailer truck. Its tail measures ten feet from top to bottom—that's as tall as the height at which a basketball hoop is mounted. Despite its size, the whale shark is harmless to humans. In fact, scuba divers sometimes hitch a free ride on the shark's back or by holding on to one of its fins.

The whale shark is like a whale in more ways than its size. Like some of the largest whales, the whale shark is a filter-feeder. This giant water strainer opens its six-foot-wide mouth and filters plankton and even entire schools of small fish from thousands of tons of seawater each hour.

Whale sharks live in both tropical and temperate ocean waters, usually far out at sea. They usually swim alone, but some groups of up to a dozen whale sharks swimming together have been sighted.

The hammerhead shark is one of the most unusual-looking fish in the sea. Its wide, flattened snout really does look like the head of a hammer. Its eyes and nostrils are at the outermost tips of the hammerhead. By swinging its head back and forth as it swims, a hammerhead gets a wide view of its surroundings.

There are about nine different kinds of hammerheads, ranging in length from four feet to twenty feet. Several of the largest kinds, including the scalloped hammerhead, the smooth hammerhead, and the great hammerhead, are fairly common in North American waters. These large hammerheads are dangerous hunters but live mainly in offshore coastal waters and feed on fish, including other sharks. Sometimes hammerheads come into shallow waters to feed and have been known to attack humans when they do.

Most hammerheads are solitary swimmers. But scalloped hammerheads (shown here) often swim in groups of up to 100 sharks. Scientists are not sure why they do this. Hammerheads have few natural enemies, so protection doesn't seem to be a good explanation for this behavior. Perhaps they gather together because of abundant food in the area or for reproductive purposes.

Probably the best known of all sharks is the great white shark. It is the third largest shark, but the most dangerous. In the movie *Jaws*, the great white was pictured as a fierce, intelligent, and unpredictable human-eating monster. But "human biting" is probably more accurate, because only rarely does a great white—or any other shark—actually eat people.

When it does attack humans, the great white shark probably mistakes the swimmer for a sea lion or seal, its favorite food. After a bite or two the shark discovers the person isn't a seal and swims away. This isn't to say that the great white isn't dangerous. Even a single bite can cause great loss of blood, shock, and death. The jaws of a great white shark are filled with fifty two-and-one-half-inch pointed teeth—the largest teeth of any shark. Narrow teeth on the bottom jaw hold the prey while the saw-edged teeth on top cut it into bite-sized chunks.

Unlike most fish and many sharks, the great white is warm-bodied—which is not the same as warm-blooded. The great white has a body temperature as much as ten degrees Fahrenheit warmer than the surrounding water. This warmer body temperature means more energy so the shark can swim faster and catch its prey more easily.

Sharks don't attack people very often, but by following these simple rules you can reduce your risk of an attack even further.

- Don't swim in water when sharks have been seen, especially in places where garbage or waste is dumped. Sharks often stay in an area for several weeks.

- Always swim with another person or in a group. Sharks are more likely to attack lone swimmers.

- If you have a cut, stay out of the water until it stops bleeding.

- Sharks are more likely to attack bright or shiny objects, so it's probably wise to remove jewelry before you go swimming.

- If you do see a shark, don't panic. The more you splash around, the more interested the shark will be in you. Tuck your arms and legs toward your body and try to keep still.

Sharks have been swimming the oceans for longer than people have even existed. The earliest known sharks lived more than 400 million years ago. That was 200 million years before the first dinosaurs. Rather than thinking of sharks as monsters to be destroyed, we can learn to appreciate their interesting lives. If we understand their behavior, we can avoid most dangerous encounters and live in harmony with these most awesome fish.